Historic Spring City

A National Historic District Tour Guide Book

Compiled by Cherrie Barrow

Edited by Kaye C. Watson

Cover photo by Cherrie Barrow, 2016

Published by The Picket Fence Co., LLC for

Canal Creek Camp

Daughters of Utah Pioneers

ACKNOWLEDGEMENT

The information for this book has been taken from *Life Under the Horseshoe: A History of Spring City* which was published by the Spring City Daughters of Utah Pioneers in 1987 with the help of Spring City Corporation. (No effort has been made to cite the page for reference in this work, however, all credit should be given to the original researchers and contributors.) Additional information has been gleaned from pioneer histories contributed to our DUP Camp library. This booklet was inspired by previously published editions of Spring City tour booklets, first publication in 1984 by the DUP for the first Heritage Day Home Tour event.

The descriptions of the houses were supplied by Kaye Watson from Dr. Tom Carter's application for Spring City to be listed on the National Historic Register in 1978. A few photos have been scanned from *Life Under the Horseshoe*, or from our DUP camp library. Front cover photo by Cherrie Barrow, as well as all current photos.

It is the objective of Daughters of Utah Pioneers to honor those who have gone before, remembering their lives, and teaching lessons of faith, courage, fortitude, and patriotism (International Society Daughters of Utah Pioneers handbook). The proceeds from this book will help promote historic Spring City and preserve our heritage.

CANAL CREEK CAMP
DAUGHTERS OF UTAH PIONEERS

As Daughters of Utah Pioneers in Spring City, we are fortunate to have the stewardship of three museum sites in our town. These museums preserve historical artifacts, house pioneer histories of those who settled Spring City, and help promote the history of the town. We are a non-profit, historical organization and depend on donations and volunteerism.

Old City Hall Museum

Old Jail Museum

Old School Community Center

A BRIEF HISTORY

When James Allred and his family arrived in Utah in the fall of 1851, the little village of Manti was the only Sanpete settlement in existence, having been settled in November 1849. President Young suggested James select a place for settlement in this long mountain valley. In March 1852, James Allred, his wife Elizabeth, their family and a few others settled along "Canal Creek," about 17 miles north of Manti and it became known as the Allred Settlement.

Despite Chief Wakara's invitation to settle the San Pitch valley, there were "troubles" with the Ute warriors. Although the settlement was bolstered by about 50 Danish families in the fall of 1853, they had to abandon their little town for the safety of Manti in December.

The Walker War ended in 1854, although the underlying issues were not solved, and gradually the overcrowded pioneers began to venture out again to their old settlements. Most of the Allred Settlement families moved to Cottonwood Creek and built Fort Ephraim. In July 1859, William Y. Black requested and received President Young's approval to resettle "Little Denmark." "Spring Town" was born as Father Black's little group was quickly joined by the Allreds and grew from the anticipated 30 families to a population of more than 220 in the 1860 Census. Life was very difficult in the 1860s with much home building, land clearing, and planting to support the increasing population amid the outbreak of the Blackhawk War. Black Hawk died in 1870, but it was two more years before hostilities came to a close. Finally, the pioneers in the 1870s and 1880s were able to build, businesses developed, and the town flourished. "Spring City" was incorporated in 1870.

The Danes and other Scandinavians settled primarily in the northern part of town. Their dwellings were a marked contrast to the 1½ story Mormon-style homes in the southern part of town. Many Danes built homes like those in their native land: long and low in appearance with doors and windows symmetrically arranged in the façade. Chimneys were often built in the center as opposed to the gable-end chimneys characteristic of the Mormon-style home. Outbuildings, often of rock, were constructed in close proximity to the home or were sometimes attached. Thatching was a common roofing material. Woven willow fences were erected, but were not widespread.

The first generation Danish immigrants also differed from the other settlers in that they almost all had a trade. Most Danes were not involved in livestock operations, but had only a cow, a few chickens, pigs, and a garden. They were not sheepmen or farmers on much more than a subsistence level. Instead, most Danes were blacksmiths, bakers, wheelwrights, coopers, shoemakers, carpenters, masons, and tinkers. These craftsmen made a valuable contribution to the building of the community.

A PIONEER VILLAGE

At one time, nearly every home in town possessed their own milk cow, chickens, horses, and probably a few sheep and pigs. The large lots most certainly had a large garden and fruit trees, a root cellar, granary, barns, sheds, an outhouse, and other outbuildings. The streets are wide and laid out in a grid plan with the once thriving business district on the main street. The farmland was located outside the city limits thus promoting a feeling of community with social and educational opportunities within the town.

Spring City still reflects what life was like in a 19th Century Mormon Village. The town received the designation of "National Historic District" October 22, 1980. Fortunately, home owners are proud of the town's heritage and many of the homes are preserved.

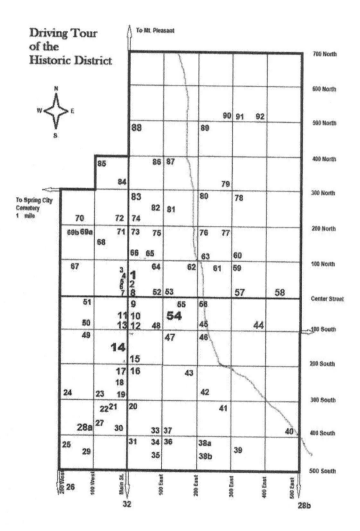

Driving Tour of the Historic District

To Mt. Pleasant

NO. I
Old City Hall, 1893
46 North Main

The old City Hall is one of the few surviving vernacular civic buildings remaining in Sanpete County. Built of local oolite limestone, it is a temple form building with a bell tower. Construction was begun in 1890 and the building completed in 1893. Community craftsmen included stonemasons Jens J. "Rock" Sorensen, John F. Bohlin, and Jens Carlson and carpenters William Downard, Marenus Mortensen, and Lars Larsen. Other craftsmen probably also contributed their skills.

It was used as a schoolhouse until 1900 when the large public school was opened. Two municipal bands used it as a practice hall. It also served as the City Hall until 1988 when this  function was moved to the old Junior High school. This building is now a Daughters of Utah Pioneers museum and Spring City information center presenting the history of the town. Family histories of the settlers submitted by Daughters of Utah Pioneers can be found here as part of the DUP library. Behind the building is an old jailhouse. Its construction date is unknown; however, it was before 1912 when it was recorded in the City minutes that the jail was in need of repairs, including a second stove and more bedding. Among the tools displayed in the old jail is a stone mason's facer tool used to score the stone used in the old City Hall giving the surface its unique pattern.

The old jail was no longer used once prisoners were able to be transported via automobile to the Manti jail. It was used as the City maintenance shed until 1988 when City Hall moved to the old Junior High. The barred windows show the stacked 2x4 construction, and an original jail cell is still there. It was converted to a museum in 2004.

NO. 2
Old Firehouse, c. 1900
44 North Main

Orson Allred built this building for commercial purposes. The Allred Hotel, across the street, often had traveling salesmen as their guests. The building has a wood frame false front and was utilized by "drummers' to display their goods to local merchants. Later, the City purchased the building and has used it for storage and as a fire engine house. This building is currently used as a research library.

NO. 3
The Allred Hotel
Crisp-Allred Home, 1881-1884
59 North Main

This large two-story hall-parlor stone house was built by James Crisp in 1884 after he became wealthy hauling freight to Nevada mining camps. Mr. Crisp suffered an untimely death due to a farming accident. The home was purchased by Orson and Lorena (Sorensen) Allred; after a few years, a hotel operation began. They built the rear addition which included five bedrooms upstairs, a larger kitchen downstairs, and the front porch.

The Hotel Log Book was donated and can be found in the Old City Hall museum. A great variety of guests were noted other than the traveling salesmen, such as teachers, politicians, newspapermen, several doctors, the 1915-16 football team, and many traveling entertainment groups. It also featured group dining; in 1915 a dinner to honor Judge Jacob Johnson upon his return from Washington was held here.

NO. 4
Sandstrom's Pool and Dance Hall, c. 1911
37 North Main

William Sandstrom built the two-story adobe-lined, wood frame building to the north side of this commercial block on Main Street south of the Allred Hotel about 1911. The gable roof is visible from behind the false front. He operated a small grocery and candy store. One pool table was located in the rear of the store, and the upstairs was used as a dance hall. When the dancers were actively engaged, the downstairs hanging lamps would also dance in unison with the floor's vibrations. Sandstrom was accidentally killed in Wyoming in June 1911, and then his wife's brother, Alvin Bertelson, operated the store for a short time selling candy and tobacco.

Later this building became the Post Office with Postmaster James W. Blain. In more recent memory it was operated as a grocery store and other businesses. It remained empty for a long time, but has now been remodeled into the unique home of Lawrence and Lana Gardner; the storefront is Lana's Sewing.

No. 5
Lyceum Theatre, 1915
35 North Main

The Lyceum Theater, later known as The Victory, was constructed by John R. Baxter, Jr. It is a brick two-part block commercial structure with a stepped gable.

In 1915 after John R. Baxter, Jr. had been in charge of the "old Blue Hall" for a short time, he and his wife Enid conceived the grand idea of a more modern theater in Spring City. Grand opening ceremonies were held July 24, 1915 with a 15-week serial. Theatricals and silent films such as "Birth of a Nation," "The Virginian," "Phantom of the Opera," "The Ten Commandments," and "Hunchback of Notre Dame" were brought to town via this theatre.

Matinee tickets were 10¢ for children and 25¢ for adults in 1918, with evening prices raised to 20¢ for children and 35¢ for adults (10% tax added WWI).

The Lyceum became the social and cultural center with a great variety of activities being held within its walls. Basketball games, roller skating, wedding receptions, plays, debates, political meetings, and chicken "feeds" with a dance afterwards, were all part of Spring City's social scene at this time.

It was operated by the Baxters until 1927 when it was sold and named "The Victory." A few years later the building became the Spring City Ward Cultural Hall and remained so until 1978 when the new church cultural hall was completed.

No. 6
The Baxter Confectionary, 1915
33 North Main

Baxter's Confectionary was a by-word for sweets for over 50 years. It was built by John R. Baxter at the

same time as the Theater and operated until 1973. For a short time in 1916 it was also used as a drug store. In 1920 a soda fountain was added and a lovely French plate glass mirror installed as a part of the fountain cabinet features. "The Shop" was divided into a front and back area by a lattice divider. Candy was on display in the front glass showcases and shelves with a longer counter where ice cream cones and drinks were served. There were two booths in the rear area with tables as well as several small round tables where customers could sit and eat their treats. A stove was located in the back where many residents gathered on cold days to warm themselves and catch up on local gossip.

Candy mostly came in wooden buckets. There were 5¢ bars. Ice cream cones were 5¢, nut Sundaes 15¢ and banana splits 25¢. In later years, the confectionary specialized in penny candy and became known as "John's Candy Store." A trip wasn't complete without going to John's Candy Store.

William Ford Home, 1880
13 North Main

William Ford built this frame and adobe lined house about 1880. The hall-parlor plan with a rear addition is typical for the area although the clapboard siding is not. Ford's blacksmith shop was likely situated to the west of the house. The house was sold to Edward Sahlburg about 1920. John Baxter, Jr., who built the Confectionary and the Lyceum Theatre, lived here for many years. John Baxter was also Mayor for 16 years, 1958-1973.

William Puzey's Wheelright was located south across Center Street from Ford's blacksmith shop. Many needy wagons were repaired by him and sent on their way so that they could continue their productivity. These two craftsmen worked together at times to build wagons, however, they mainly were occupied by repair jobs. Abram Acord was the lucky buyer of the first wagon built by Puzey and Ford.

NO. 8
Rasmus & Sarah A. Justesen Home, c. 1875
12 North Main

This 1½ story adobe house was built for Rasmus Justesen and his first wife, Sarah A. Shepherd, who raised nine children here. It was originally stuccoed and scored to resemble cut stone, including simulated quoins. His second wife was Anine Marie Larsen, and they had 10 children. She was the daughter of the first Bishop after the resettlement of 1859, Christian G. Larsen, and she accompanied Rasmus to Castle Dale. Rasmus Justesen served as 2nd Counselor in the second Bishopric (1868) with Bishop Frederick Olson.

He was active in many community activities including Mayor, Councilman, School Trustee and Patriarch. He was also one of the fifteen prominent men appointed as members of the Standing Committee for the purpose of erecting the new meetinghouse.

Artist Susan Gallacher purchased and restored the house in 2002.

John Frantzen Home, c. 1880
73 South Main

This 1½ story hall-parlor house was built by John Franzten. It is one of the few remaining adobe houses along Main Street. A Mormon convert, Frantzen emigrated from Norway in 1857, settling in Spring City in 1860. His experience may have been typical of early 1860s arrivals. He and his parents lived in a wagon box, managing to build a small log home before the spring work began. John and his father each received 13½ acres along Oak Creek. During their first spring, John "grubbed and plowed nine acres of land for (him)self, father not quite (as) much." They also were able to plant some fruit trees. "The supply of water was insufficient to mature the crops, and if it had not been for the excellent rain on the 24th of July our crops would have been an entire failure."

Active in the LDS church as 1st Counselor to the Spring City Bishop for 15 years. He was a practicing polygamist with two wives and served a jail term for cohabitation. It is likely that one room of the house served as the first store in town.

Everett Strate's Garage, c. 1919-1962
53 South Main

The old Johnson's Merc, formerly the Young Men's Co-op probably was demolished to make room for the Strate's Garage ca. 1919. A. Everett Strate, born in 1897, was a natural mechanic who had a flair for repairing all types of machinery. The first automobiles came to town about 1915.

Everett Strate sold Pontiac and Oldsmobiles, and other cars, Goodyear and Firestone tires, batteries and

other equipment, in addition to gasoline with pumps located in front of the garage on Main Street. Massey-Harris tractors were also for sale for a few years. When it became available, he bought a home near the garage (north). At one time a liquor outlet also operated in the garage, but was taken out because of employee problems. When Everett passed away in 1961 the garage passed to his sons; however, it soon closed because of the prevailing economic conditions and other problems. The building is currently the Spring City Arts Gallery.

Osborne Mercantile, 1930
Currently, The Soda Fountain.
76 South Main

Isaac Edgar Allred owned and operated a drug store in the same location as the Osborne's Mercantile, later known as the Horseshoe Grocery building. It intermittently sat vacant until purchased for The Soda Fountain.

Allred's drug store was constructed of lumber; previously, he had a small candy store south of the saloon. He made his own ice cream and root beer, along with any medicines ordered by local doctors for people or animals. A Post

Office was erected south of the drug store and was used at different times by Charlie "Watchmaker" Nelson for his watch repair business. A barber was also located there at one time, and later Allred's soda fountain tables. Next door, to the north of Allred's Drug Store, was Beck's Mercantile, once the Johnson Mercantile which burned in July 1929.

The Allred Drug was purchased by Pratt Osborne who operated it as a store for a few years. After the neighboring fire, the old wooden store was torn down and the new brick building constructed in 1930.

No. 12
Paul & Charles Kofford Home, c. 1860
11 East 100 South

One of Spring City's earliest stone houses was built for Paul E. Kofford by stonemason Peter Olsen Hansen. The house plan is uncommon with a front facing parlor followed by two rooms at the rear. Paul's son Charles acquired the house and resided there for many years. The house was renovated and restored in 2005.

Paul Kofford was a translator between Scandinavian immigrants of Spring City and the English-speaking pioneers. He had been a sea captain and could understand the Danish language. Life in the Spring Town fort during the war years held a variety of activities including the baking of bread in Mother Kofford's "large Dutch oven made of adobe" where the town's women attended to this chore. Fanny Kofford was a compassionate woman gifted in caring for the sick, skillful in using herbs as a medicine.

NO. 13
Mary Ann Pollard Allred, 1909
90 South Main

Mary Ann Pollard Allred was the third wife of James Anderson Allred. Their first home was at 297 South 100 West, #23. This is a 1½ story brick pattern book house. It is an excellent example of the prevailing architectural fashion in Spring City during the "turn-of-the-century" period. This house replaced an older two-room adobe structure built by Louis Lund.

Mary Ann's family joined the LDS Church in England and they arrived in Salt Lake valley in 1857. She became a plural wife of James A. Allred in 1866 and had six children. Her husband, Bishop James A. Allred passed away in 1904. Mary Ann built this house in 1909. She was living in Salt Lake when she died in 1930.

NO. I4
Spring City LDS Chapel, I897-I9II
I64 South Main

The Chapel construction was begun under the direction of Bishop James A. Allred and completed under Bishop Lauritz O. Larsen. It was designed by architect Richard C. Watkins of Provo, and by mid-1890s the foundation was underway. It was built of oolitic limestone quarried in the hills south of town.

Masons Jens J. Carlson, Jens Sorensen and Lars Larsen worked under the supervision of John F. Bohlin. The principal carpenters were Emil Erickson and, from Mt. Pleasant, George Brand and George Ryland. The building was completed at a cost of $40,000 with $34,000 being raised by local donation and labor. The annex was constructed  by Charles and Nephi Christensen. The Chapel was dedicated by Anton H. Lund March 15, 1914.

The building features Gothic arched windows and recessed main face with a 75 ft. square entrance tower topped by an octagonal spire. The vaulted and beamed interior slopes to the pulpit on the west with handmade rostrum chairs, all with skillfully carved woodwork, as are the pew ends and sacrament table. The annex was originally entered through hand-grained sliding doors behind the pulpit with a baptismal font below. The unique, self-supporting curved horseshoe gallery is accessed from the tower providing an impressive view of the Chapel. The wooden benches were purchased from Dinwoody's furniture in Salt Lake City at a cost of $1300.

Although the Chapel received some remodeling in 1929, 1939 and the 1950s, it was under Bishop Osral Allred's direction that the Chapel received the remodel and addition of the cultural hall wing mid-1970s. The stone was quarried at the original site in the first Pigeon Hollow, transported to Salt Lake and finished by Hansen Stone Contractors. After being cut and numbered, it was hauled back to Spring City during 1975. Ward members willingly contracted to complete site clearing, excavation, painting, electrical work, trusses and roofing, tree removal, millwork, landscaping, cabinets, etc. A local carpenter, Claude Acord, completed the beautiful carved wooden staircase just inside the doors of the addition.

This Chapel has the distinction of being the LDS Church's first preservation and addition to an historic Chapel rather than replacing it with a new building. It was dedicated August 6, 1978 and is now listed among the Church's top 15 historic buildings. The Chapel has been found to be acoustically near-perfect and has brought an added cultural dimension to Spring City.

Niels H. Borresen Home, c. 1864
197 South Main

Niels Borresen was converted to the LDS church in Denmark and came to Utah in the late 1850s; he moved to Spring City in 1860. This is one of the oldest stone houses in Spring City. It was constructed of two-foot thick random rubble stone. The wood-frame addition was constructed in 1994.

Niels Borreson was a multi-talented craftsman who was trained as a horticulturalist and was also Spring City's "leading miller for many years." Borresen would plant orchards and sell young fruit trees and plants to anyone who needed them. His *Pyramid* death notice recorded that "he was the first man to ever plant an apple tree in Mt. Pleasant."

During the Blackhawk War, Peter Borresen, son of Niels H., was one of the boys who went quickly to the top of the old meeting house in the fort area across the street to beat a drum to warn outside workers of approaching "Indians."

NO. 16
Orson Hyde Home, c. 1868
209 South Main

Orson Hyde served a number of missions in the early years of the Church, and became one of the Twelve Apostles in 1835. In 1840, he dedicated Palestine to the return of the Jews. When the Mormons began their westward trek, he and his family remained at Winter Quarters for a few years to help other evacuees and arrived in the Salt Lake Valley in 1852. In 1860 he was called to preside in Sanpete.

The Hyde's first home was of hewn logs on the block west, which his family soon outgrew. This impressive rock home was built after 1864 of oolitic limestone standing 2½ stories tall with walls 20" thick. The staircase in the center of the home angles several times, with landings, as it ascends to the attic floor. The full floors have four rooms. The floors contained random-width boards. In the main rooms, the rich brown finish on the window and door casings had been hand-grained with stiff feathers.

A spring provided cool storage in the half basement, similar to that in his log home. The water came into the basement through a pipe on the south side near the front wall; it ran along in a shallow cement ditch and out the front near the other side (Hyde). There are two original limestone outbuildings and a part of a large barn on the property. The wood frame addition to the rear of the house is more recent.

NO. 17
William & Margaret Osborne Home, 1894
The Osborne Inn
216 South Main

The Osborne house is a fine example of Victorian pattern book architecture in Sanpete County. The 1½ story brick cross-wing house has shingled gables, intricately bracketed eaves, corbelled relieving arches, and polychrome brick. Originally, there was a circular turret above the south porch.

Margaret (Beck) Osborne began operating it as a hotel around 1896. Although most of their customers were reputable, such as traveling salesmen, Margaret also fed local men who were arrested and bedded overnight on the Osborne Hotel floors.

William Osborne was a merchant who owned a meat shop and confectionery shop once located just north of the chapel.

No. 18
Arthur Johnson Meat Market, c. 1905
Horseshoe Mountain Pottery
278 South Main

This small brick building with a false front was built in 1905 by Alvin E. Allred, the son of Isaac M. Allred. It is believed that it was a Confectionary and Pool Hall. The building is a two-part block, false front commercial structure. The gambrel roof replaced an earlier gable roof. Alvin spent his early years working at the sawmill in Canal Canyon and was well-known as a singer; he managed the Opera House.

The Johnson Meat Market was operated by Arthur Johnson, son of Judge Johnson, about 1916. He mainly sold meats, but also had a few grocery items for sale. This building stood unoccupied for years, but was also used as a home before being purchased by Joe Bennion, who has somewhat enlarged it for his pottery operation adding several potter's kilns located behind the building.

NO. 19
Neils Adler Home, c. 1875
296 South Main

This 1½ story yellow brick house was one of the first fired brick houses in Spring City. It is a hall-parlor plan with a rear 1890s lean-to addition. Neils was an early Utah immigrant from Sweden serving as cook in his company. He came to Spring Town by 1867 and raised six children in this home. He served a Scandinavian mission. Neils died at the age of 93 in Castle Dale, Utah.

A brick-making operation was located east of the Spring City Cemetery; its operator was John H. A. Strate, an emigrant of German extraction who came here about 1874 from Denmark where he had been a baker. After coming to Spring City, he settled on the bend of the road near the current site of Strate's Pond (UT117) and lived in a log house. John engaged in the brick-making business, casting adobe from the mud of the creek in the little ravine out there. His children recalled how exacting he was about the mixture of mud and straw that went into the molds. He also provided hand-molded sand-rolled bricks which were fired in a kiln "in the second holler." To this day when the fields are worked more bricks keep turning up.

Lauritz Larsen Home, c. 1860s
12 East 300 South

Lauritz Larsen constructed this adobe hall-parlor house in the 1860s. The house was later sheathed with stucco, as are most adobe homes, in order to protect

the soft adobe bricks from the weather. He was born in 1834 in Denmark, arrived in Utah in 1857 and settled in Spring Town. He became 2nd Counselor to Bishop James A. Allred. Lauritz is the first known LDS missionary to leave Spring Town for a foreign mission, 1867-1870. He was twice elected Mayor of Spring City, and in 1892 he served as a member of the Utah Constitutional Convention. A farmer, he was also Justice of the Peace. Lauritz passed away in Spring City in 1895, and the house passed to his son L. O. Larsen, who also served as Mayor, and as Bishop from 1904 until his death in 1913. Although our chapel was completed during his bishopric, it was not dedicated until after his death.

Later, Ernest B. Terry, the town music teacher, acquired the house. It eventually became the home and studio of notable Sanpete artist Ella Peacock.

NO. 2I
John Frank Allred Schoolhouse, I876
AKA the "Endowment House"
63 West 300 South

The cornerstone for a Relief Society hall was laid in 1870, but as funds were needed for the construction of the Manti Temple, this one-story, temple form, Greek Revival style building wasn't constructed until about 1876. It was known as the "John Frank Allred School" and was used as a school for 20 years. It was believed to also have been the office of Orson Hyde;

 the two years prior to it becoming a school it may have been used for endowments. "O. Hyde's office" in Spring City is mentioned as the site where endowments were carried out, but the building was not constructed for that purpose. One of Hyde's grandson's, Barney, has stated that the "Mormon" markings were placed there by a local man in mockery of the Church. These markings were removed from this building and it is now a private home.

Orson Hyde died in 1878, and the building was sold to the Spring City School District. It remained a school until 1899 when the Spring City Public School was completed. The building was purchased and restored by artist Randall Lake in 1982.

No. 22
Relief Society Granary, c. 1870-76
69 West 300 South

In 1868 the "Female Relief Society of Springtown" was organized with Mary Ann Price Hyde as President. The school and the granary were built of oolite limestone. These structures were built on land belonging to Mary Ann Hyde, trustee for the Relief Society. The granary was completed and used as the office as well as for meetings. After 1911 the old adobe meetinghouse south of the rock Chapel on Main Street was used.

The Relief Society women were able to achieve many worthy goals with limited money and resources; for example, they gathered Sunday eggs so that they could make a donation to the Manti Temple building fund. It was said that most chickens in town were highly cooperative and laid more Sunday eggs than they did during the weekdays. A total of $800 in cash was donated by our women, along with many beautiful handmade articles and food for the Temple workers. As new Saints arrived, there was "much gleaning done and wheat stored."

NO. 23
James Anderson Allred Home, 1874
297 South 100 West

James A. Allred was the son of William and Sarah (Warren) Allred. He was a rather wealthy man when he arrived in Salt Lake in 1861 with a large caravan of wagons, herds and supplies. He and his family were "called" to go to Sanpete in 1865 to help build up the area. He built this two-story Federal style  frame house of California redwood in 1874. It is a central-passage plan, unusual in Spring City, and has a rear addition. Adjacent to the house is a stone root cellar with gabled bulwark entrance, and a framed "inside-out granary; both date from the 1870s. Two of Allred's wives lived here and raised six children. It was purchased by William Osborne in 1909.

After James' arrival in Spring Town, he spent much time with Orson Hyde, accompanying him on numerous trips through southern Utah. James served a number of years as First Counselor to Bishop Fred Olson and became Bishop in 1882 and served until his death in 1904. In 1870, he was elected Spring City's first Mayor, serving five consecutive two-year terms. He also served one term as County Commissioner and several terms as Probate Judge.

NO. 24
Jacob Nielsen Log Cabin, c. 1870
289 South 200 West

This cabin was built by Jacob Nielsen in the 1870s. It is built of logs hewn on top and bottom and joined at the corners with a "V" notch. The adjacent stone granary was built about 1875. The wood frame and clapboard addition at the rear of the cabin was added in the 1990s. The cabin originally faced 300 So.

Jacob and his wife, Ellen, arrived in America in 1868. They had lost three of their eight children in Denmark, and three more in the New York harbor. Then, their son, Ole, drowned in the Spanish Fork River. Jacob was a blacksmith and heard blacksmiths were needed in Sanpete, so they moved to Spring City, bought land and built their home with a blacksmith shop on the west part of the lot. After Jacob's death in 1908, grandson Alfred and his wife cared for Ellen until her death in 1914. Their son, Hans, bought the home.

No. 25
Soren Larsen, Jr. Home, c. 1899
441 South 200 West

This home is an excellent example of one of the most common folk house types encountered in Spring City. It certainly dates from the later 19th Century and dramatically illustrates the persistence of older house forms in the area. It is a one-story, three opening hall-

parlor type folk design. It has been renovated in recent years.

Soren and Maria met and married at sea. They were so happy not to have to stay in Denmark and marveled at the sights of "Indians" and buffalo. They arrived in Salt Lake in 1854 with a company of Scandinavian immigrants; they moved to Ephraim in 1858, and Spring City in 1862. Soren, a Dane who fought for his country against Germany, was a "Minute Man" during the Blackhawk War. He declared ownership of this fertile lot on Canal Creek in 1869 rather than joining his countrymen in the northern part of town. He was a farmer and a good carpenter who made his own furniture. His son, Soren, Jr. built this house on the lot of his father's adobe home and where many of his children were born.

William Major, Jr. Home, c. 1875
527 South 200 West

This house is one of the earliest large rock homes in town. It is a 1½ story stone hall-parlor house with rear "T" kitchen on the east. This house is architecturally significant as an outstanding example of the 19th century Mormon folk architecture.

Sarah (Coles) Major Ellis lost her first husband, William Major, while he was serving an English  mission. She then married Joseph T. Ellis, and they arrived in Spring Town shortly after Buchanan's army entered Utah. Joseph T. Ellis was among the first families to resettle the town in 1859. They chose 15 acres of land on the southwest corner of town. Sarah's son, William Major, Jr. married Ellen Meek, daughter of James Meek who was killed at the stone quarry by the Utes during a raid on the town in 1867. William built this rock home after learning how to cut and shape stone on the Manti Temple. It is still owned by descendants of William Major.

They had an adobe yard just north of the house by the waters of Canal Creek where Vince Major made adobe bricks of the clay soil as late as the 1930s.

NO. 27
Jens Peter Carlson Home, c. 1896
350 South 100 West

This 1½ story Victorian eclectic cross-wing house is noteworthy for the craftsmanship of its ashlar stone masonry. No other residence in Sanpete County exhibits the high level of masonry which Jens, lavished on this house. Local tradition suggests the house was something of a showcase for Carlson's considerable talents as a stone mason and that its construction was precipitated by a rivalry between Carlson and his neighbor, Judge Jacob Johnson.

It seems that Johnson hired a Salt Lake firm to design and build the addition to his home in the early 1890s. Once construction was underway, Carlson was appalled at the quality of the workmanship, and so he determined to demonstrate the potential of a rock home. Work on the house was initiated in 1896 and he labored on it for the next eight years, but the two-story house was never completed. Only the Manti Temple rivals the Carlson house for excellence in masonry. The stones were rubbed together to achieve a smooth finish, and the filings were mixed with lime for the $1/8^{th}$ mortar. Even interior walls are of stone.

No. 28●
Judge Jacob Johnson Home, c. 1875, 1896
390 South 100 West

This is the largest historic home in Spring City and consists of two distinct styles. The south section of the building was the original stone structure; it was built after 1875. It is a classical two-story hall-parlor building. In 1896 the large Victorian addition was built complete with a circular corner tower and conical roof. The stone building to the north of the house was the Judge's office; a fine stone granary and a large stone carriage house were also built on the property.

Jacob Johnson was a local man of note. He was born in 1847 in Denmark and arrived in Ogden with his mother in 1856. She left the Church because of polygamy and married a Morrisite, Mr. Smith, whose cruelty to his step-sons caused Jacob to go to California at about age 15, where he arrived about two months later. He picked up some odd jobs and then worked in a law office, later attending Berkeley and passing the Bar examination. Other business ventures included mining with some friends in Carson City 1869, White Pine and Elko, Nevada, and becoming the Deputy Sheriff in Elko County for 18 months.

Jacob married and moved to Spring City about 1873 to homestead and to begin a law practice. He was City Attorney for nearly all the towns in the area, notary public for several years and District Attorney for 1½ terms. In 1895 he became Probate Judge, and was also a member of the Territorial Legislature, as well as U.S. Commissioner and Assistant to the U.S. District Attorney. In 1912, Johnson successfully ran for U.S. Congress where he served for two years.

Johnson invested in a great many Spring City's commercial ventures such as the Creamery, flour mill, opera house, Young Men's Co-op and the Horseshoe Canal Company. He also contributed money to the LDS Chapel fund and aided the poor of the town whenever possible. He even acted as banker to those in need of financial assistance.

NO. 28b
Jacob Johnson Farmhouse, c. 1876
3.1 miles SE of town on Canal Canyon Rd.

Jacob Johnson homesteaded 160 acres on this site and lived here five years before applying to acquire the property under the Homestead Act of 1881. He built this three-room rock home and eventually acquired an additional 640 acres, clearing and planting crops, much of which he shared with his less fortunate neighbors and friends. This farm-house with a view was restored in 2001 by Carl, Jeanie Timm.

NO. 29
Justesen-Olsen Home, c. 1876
428 South 100 West

A one-story hall-parlor house built with the assistance of mason Jens "Rock" Sorensen for Peter Justesen. It was sold in 1877 to Matilda Justesen Olsen whose daughter, Matilda F. Justesen Johnson,

inherited the house in 1893 and sold it to James W. Blain in 1913. His brother, Max Blain, a local artist, lived here for many years. Matilda F.'s father was Lars Alexander Justesen who was killed by Indians in an attack at Rocky Ford along the Sevier River in 1868. Judge Johnson's first wife died in 1884. He then married Matilda F. Justesen in 1885, but she did not live here.

James W. Blain was the Principal at the Spring City Elementary School, and then at the Jr. High School. In his history, he relates how when he and his wife, Dorcas Allred, married in 1903 they lived the first three years of their marriage in a "house" on John T. Blain's property, that of his father William Blain on Main Street across from the spring. "...we lived in John Thomas' chicken coop. He had a place right across from the spring, but somebody had raised chickens in it. We cleaned what feathers we could get out..."

Thomas Schroder/Samuel Allred Home, 1876
390 South Main

This 1½ story stone hall-parlor house was built by Thomas G. Schroder, a German convert to the LDS church. Samuel Allred purchased the house from Schroder in 1878 and added a wing to the rear of the

house about 1900.

Samuel was born in 1851 in Council Bluffs, the son of Isaac and Mary Allred; his father was the captain of 50 wagons who came to Salt Lake in 1851. Samuel and his first wife, Elizabeth, lived in this house.

When he was 15 years of age, he was an express rider who was chased by "Indians" many times. He was a courageous rider and very knowledgeable about their trickery, thus escaping death many times. At the outbreak of the Blackhawk War, he took the awful news to Ephraim. As a boy, he hauled some of the first rock used for the temple. He was noted for his natural abilities in caring for the sick and wounded.

Samuel was Bishop at the time the new rock Chapel was dedicated, and was the first man to offer a formal prayer within its walls.

NO. 31
Reuben Warren Allred Home, 1864
415 South Main

Reuben Warren Allred, Sr. built the original stone section of this house in 1864. The older section faced north and was a three-opening rectangular cabin type house with a central partition. The upstairs loft was reached by an outside staircase.

The brick rear "T" was added in 1909 by his son Warren Allred. Warren's daughter, Tessie Pyper and her husband purchased the home in 1975 and altered it severely, blocking up the north door and plastering the exterior. A summer kitchen originally set directly behind the house to the south, but was moved when

the brick portion was added. A large log barn sat directly to the south; it is now dismantled.

Reuben Warren Allred was the son of town founders James and Elizabeth Warren Allred. He was a farmer, a blacksmith, and a ropemaker. Reuben was the first Bishop of the little settlement and when the Indian troubles started, he and his father traveled to October Conference 1853 making the request of Brigham Young for additional families which resulted in 50 Danish families joining them, becoming known as "Little Denmark."

NO. 32
Charles Crawforth Farmstead, c. 1884
2 miles south of town on Crawford Lane

This stately rock home was built by Charles Crawforth, a two-story hall-parlor house with a rear stone wing. Charles also worked on the construction of the Manti Temple. He was a former coachman in England and had an interest in horticulture; he came to Spring City in 1874.

The house faces north with a grand view of Mt. Nebo to the northwest. Surrounding outbuildings included a barn, stone carriage house and a stone root cellar. All were restored in  1990 by interior designer J. Scott Anderson.

An English gardener with an extremely effective green thumb, his home was surrounded by "what you'd call a paradise... he raised every kind of fruit people wouldn't even think of trying to raise now." "Indians" stole watermelons and cantaloupes from him which he piled near his home. He raised broom corn which he used to make brooms for local sale. He became a farmer and also maintained an orchard of 250 trees west of the house as well as his beautiful garden complete with peacocks. He was known to work with his bees and never wear a veil.

No. 33
John & Emma (Lucas) Robinson Home, c. 1875
95 East 400 South

John and Emma came to America in 1856 and traveled by handcart with the first Mormon Handcart  Co. suffering many hardships on the nine week journey. The family settled in Spring City in 1861. John was a gunsmith and was kept busy during the Blackhawk War repairing old guns—and after the war he became friends with the "Indians" repairing their guns as well. He built a log home which is now a small 1½ story hall-parlor house, with a rear addition. In the 1890s, he willed the house to his son, William. A parlor, kitchen and pantry were added about the turn of the 20th century, and more recently, a major addition of similar form was added.

Emma was a talented milliner and made many beautiful hats for the town ladies. She went to Salt Lake each fall and spring for Conference in a mule-drawn cart and shopped for 'artificials' with which to trim her hats and bonnets. She served as a midwife, assisting with many a birth, dearly loved by all, being so kind and gentle, with those who were ill and in need of skilled care and attention.

James T.S. Allred Home, 1864
96 East 400 South

The original cabin is the oldest house in Spring City. James T.S. Allred, a son of founder James Allred, constructed the original portion of this house from sawn logs. He was an original settler of Manti in 1849 where he built this cabin. When his father and family were called to help settle Sanpete, James T.S. moved his family and his cabin from Manti by ox team to the Canal settlement in 1852. It is in this general area along 400 South near Canal Creek where many of the Allreds built their homes. When the Walker War broke out, he was forced to move back to Manti and

over the years James T.S. moved his cabin seven times. It was sixteen feet square and could be readily assembled. After the town was resettled in 1859, he returned along with other original settlers. Today, the log cabin is covered with siding.

James T.S. learned the "Indian" language, they had great respect for him and called him "Showritz". He was not always successful in calming the "Indians." It became necessary for him to serve in the Blackhawk War where he was a Major, and the Captain of the "Minute Men" at the Allred Settlement.

NO. 35
Edward F. Allred Home, c. 1890
450 South 100 East

This 1½ story oolitic limestone home was constructed on the site of founder James Allred's first cabin. Edward Francis Allred was a son of James T.S. Allred and Elizabeth Manwaring; both parents were members of the Mormon Battalion. Even though Eliza was four month pregnant, she felt she would rather suffer the hardships with her husband than continue on with the Saints. Since James T.S. did not have a wagon, she walked all the way.

Edward is said to be the first white child born in Las Vegas—it was then New Mexico Territory. James T.S. had been called to go to Las Vegas in his capacity of "Indian" interpreter. The family returned to Utah joining the rest of the Allred family in Ephraim. Soon James T.S. was again called to act as interpreter in 1864, this time to Circle Valley (Circleville) where Elizabeth died. This was a dangerous time, just before the Blackhawk War broke out.

Moving to Spring City, Edward became a farmer, and also worked in the early lumber industry getting materials for the construction of the Manti Temple. (AllredFamily. com)

37

NO. 36
Wiley Payne Allred Home, c. 1878/86
413 South 100 East

The original stone section was built between 1878 and 1886 with a later addition constructed in 1915 consisting of a bay window and a brick "L" at the rear. James R. Watson bought the property in 1894 and it

remained in the Watson family until the 1980s.

Wiley Payne Allred was a son of founder James Allred arriving in Utah in 1851. He lived in Spring Town for about three years after its resettlement then moved to Fountain Green in 1862. He was a stonecutter by trade and contributed to the building of the Manti Temple, but was also set apart by Joseph Smith as a physician and gave him a doctor's book. He was a natural healer; he knew herbs and was able to use them for medicinal purposes. He was adept at the setting of broken bones. His first wife was Sarah E. Zabriskie, and he was also married to Elizabeth Davis, Johanna Olsen, and Caroline A. Fredricksen. Wiley died in Emery in 1912 where he is buried.

NO. 37
Moroni Brough Home, 1909
383 South 100 East

Moroni Brough immigrated to Utah in 1853, but because of unsettling problems with the Utes during this period they didn't move to Spring City until 1860. He married Mary Crawforth and they first lived near her father's rock home south of town for eight years where he was a farmer and raised sheep on the hillsides to the west. Although Mary suffered from the effects of scarlet fever all her life, she worked hard and was known for the readiness with which she always offered to help anyone in need.

In order to be closer to the school, Moroni built this 1½ story house of yellow brick manufactured in Manti. It is a good example of the combination of an older folk style, front gable façade with an irregular floor plan of pattern book origin. The addition to the east and a kitchen to the north were constructed in 1981 to match the original design by the owners Joe and Lee Bennion. The home is currently owned by David and Billy Tuttle. The 1880 log cabin guesthouse was originally located on Highway 117 west of town and relocated here in 1990 to serve as a studio for Lee.

No. 38●
John Franklin Allred Home, c. 1878
218 East 400 South

John Frank was born in Iowa in 1851and arrived in Utah the same year. He attended school in Provo and came to Spring City in 1872 where he taught school for two years. In 1874, he married Mary K. Bunnell and moved to Manti where he taught school for two years. In 1877, they returned to Spring City and he taught school in the rock schoolhouse on Third South until 1898 when he served a two-year LDS Mission to Wisconsin. He served as Ward YMMIA Pres. for 20 years. He also served two terms to the Utah State Legislature. In 1881, he married Sarah Ellen Bunnell, his wife's sister. He also served as Pres.

of the High Priest's Quorum and a Patriarch both here and in California on a six-month mission.

He built this home for his first wife Mary K. Bunnell soon after 1878. It is a 1½ story stone dwelling with five opening hall-parlor type house. It has a stone 1½ story wing to the rear in the "T" configuration. The floor joists were of half logs which can be seen in the cellar. The home was added onto, and vacant a number of years, recently remodeled.

No. 38b
John Franklin Allred Home,
487 South 200 East

John Frank Allred built this home for his second wife, Sarah E. Bunnell, who was the sister of his first wife (the home north on the same block) whom he married in 1881. The oldest section was one room (now the north wing). The second section of the house was the large adobe addition to the south; it was a 1½ story section which then transformed the home into a 1½ story "L" plan structure, very common in Sanpete. Other additions have been added.

The sister wives' family moved to Spring Town in 1865, where their father Samuel Bunnell became a farmer and carpenter. He served three LDS Missions to Michigan. He was "called" to be a St. George Temple builder and later also on the Manti Temple working on the spiral staircase construction. He walked the 17 miles each week for three years, his family carrying on without him. He was such an even-tempered man that it was said of him that no one had ever seen him angry. Bunnells lived here for many years and it was known for its lovely gardens; current owners are the Davises.

NO. 39
Allred-Johnson Home,
469 South 300 East

This 1½ story house is a three opening façade "hall and parlor" house. The flue is on the internal partition. The rear "L" is also stone and was part of the original structure. The stone is cut blocks of oolite with some discoloration and does not extend up the gable to the ridge, now aluminum siding.

This house is important as a late 19th Century extension of an earlier vernacular house plan. It was called exceptional by Dr. Tom Carter. It was probably built about 1890 by John W. Allred, whose wife divorced him about 1899. In 1901 John H. "Miller" Johnson next owned it. Johnson was the miller at the Spring City Roller Mill which opened in 1900. Later, Margaret Griffiths (local midwife and her second husband) bought the property in 1908. They sold the house to Herman Hermansen who was also a local miller in the nearby Roller Mill. Heinz and Donna Larsen purchased the home in 1936 and lived there for the rest of their lives. It is currently owned by Brian

and Ann Stucki, who built a new rear addition in 2017 and modernized the home.

NO. 40
Chester School & Meetinghouse, c. 1892
490 East 400 South

Chester was once a thriving community three miles west of Spring City located in "the hay bottoms." This stone building served as Chester's meetinghouse and school. Paul and Ann Larsen purchased the building, which was slated to be demolished, in 1987, and it was moved to Spring City and reconstructed.

Big Ditch runs through town in a northward direction and enters from Canal Canyon. This area to the east of 500 East along Big Ditch was the location of the  Spring City Roller Mill, incorporated in 1900. Herman Hermanson and "Miller" Johnson were among the first millers in this operation.

As electricity spread throughout the country, local men had the "bright" idea of installing an electric power plant in the same building with the Roller Mill. The Spring City Light and Milling Co. was incorporated, and in 1903 it was recommended that the city buy 12 32-candle-power lights to be placed in such position as would be most favorable to lighting the street crossings, and a light bulb was soon brought into the homes of Spring City.

NO. 41
Carl Hansen Home, c. 1890
280 East 300 South

This 1½ story yellow brick cross-wing house was built by Carl Hansen. Born in Norway, Carl came to America on the ship Idaho arriving in 1874, then traveled by train to Utah. He lived with Orson Hyde's family for a while after getting to Spring City. He married Anne Kirstine Hansen in 1882; she was a midwife. He served a Scandinavian Mission in 1894, and while he was gone, she finished the house. Their home had a well until the City water system in 1936.

He was a farmer, and served as the Spring City Justice of the Peace for several years, 1902-05. He was Postmaster 1898-1905, probably in a small building south of the Young Men's Co-op (Strate's Garage). The house was restored in the 1990s, and the current owner, artist Linda Budd, added a wood frame addition.

A newspaper article in March 1909 stated that he had "been operating a knitting factory at Spring City on a small scale and has for some time been wanting to unite with the people of Ephraim in establishing a large factory in this City."

Eugene Allred Home & Old Rock Jail, 290 South 200 East

This small stone cabin-type structure served as a jail for the town's lawbreakers 1874 to 1899, particularly when Eugene Allred served as the Marshal and lived in the house nearby. The square plan has a three-opening façade with a single wooden lintel beam supporting all three openings. Eugene's home was constructed about 1894, significant as a rather typical brick builders pattern book design employed extensively in Utah during the late 19th Century. The lot was first claimed by Spring Town School District in 1869. The Mayor's deed went, however, to Joseph T. Ellis in 1876 who built a two-room stone house on the lot. Spring City acquired the land via a tax sale in 1892 and in 1893 the lot was sold to Eugene Allred. He tore down the stone dwelling and built this fashionable house. It has been altered with the addition of a new porch and siding on the southwest corner.

NO. 43
James Rasmussen (Clawson) Home, c. 1880
184 East 200 South

James was born in 1853 in Denmark, the last child of six born to Glaus Rasmussen and Anna Fredrickson. In the Danish tradition James was the son of Glaus (Glaus-son or Claw-son). James' father died when he was about two years old, and his mother first sent her two oldest children with Elders to Zion in 1859. Three years later, a friend sponsored Anna  and her three other children; she arrived in 1862, moving her family to Spring Town, where they obtained a lot on which to build a home.

James worked hard at being a good farmer. He married Sarah Larsen and they lived in a one-room log cabin until it could be replaced with a two-room adobe home. It was later remodeled and added onto becoming this six-room home. They had good out-buildings on this lot, a great well, and the little root cellar is still located to the south of the house. Adobe bricks deteriorate with moisture, so this home was stuccoed red, and in a popular building technique in Sanpete County, it was then scored and highlighted with white paint to simulate red brick. After being vacant for many years, it was restored in 2003.

No. 44
John Blain Home, c. 1880
385 East 100 South

This 1½ story ashlar stone, hall-parlor house was built by John Blain for his family. It has a central gable indicative of the Gothic Revival style, and this dwelling is one of the finest examples of pioneer architecture in Utah. The  high level of craftsmanship and its design make it a significant example of residential architecture in Spring City. The west wing was designed to match the architecture of the original structure by new owners after 1988.

John and his wife, Serilda, lived here until their deaths. He arrived in Salt Lake with his widowed mother, Isabella Graham Blain, in 1863. His mother earned her living as "the yeast lady." Serilda's English spinning wheel can be seen in the Old School DUP museum room. When John was a very young man he worked for Orson Hyde caring for his fine horses. He was awakened one night, and seeing fires on the mountains to the west was able to warn Elder Hyde of the "Indian" raid the next day. He was one of the last survivors of the Blackhawk War veterans. He was a farmer, builder, hauled logs for lumber, and in later years did the milk route to the creamery west of town.

No. 45
Olsen-Justesen Home, c. 1888
93 South 200 East

This adobe, hall-parlor house with a symmetrical façade features gable end chimneys with elaborate corbelling and a brick rear

addition. The house was built by Lewis Olsen who sold it to Joseph Justesen, a son of Rasmus, and a local farmer and wool grower. He married Flora Geneva Hyde, daughter of Orson and Ann E. Hyde, and they raised their family here. The Elmer Olsen family purchased the home after the death of Justesen in 1960. William and Joyce Perkins renovated the house in 2005.

The Young Men's Co-op began under the ownership of Emil Erickson and Lewis Olsen in the fall of 1889. Managers through the years included Joseph A. Justesen.

NO. 46
George Downard Home, c. 1875
109 South 200 East

After immigrating to Utah in 1862, George Downard immediately located in Spring City and supported himself as a carpenter and house painter. The family moved to Richfield in the late 1860s, but soon returned and began construction of this large stone house. It is a two-story oolitic limestone hall-parlor house built in the late 1870s by George and closely resembles Orson Hyde's house in design. In 1882, George sold the house to his son, Joseph, and moved to Emery County. The house remains in the Downard family.

Their son Joseph was born in England in 1855. He devoted his life to agricultural pursuits with 200 acres of farmland. He was a stockholder in the People's Sugar Company, and served several terms on the City Council.

49

Reddick Newton Allred Home, c. 1875
115 South 100 East

Jens "Rock" Sorensen was hired to build this house. "Rock" used no scaffolding, and would place a rock on his shoulder and climb up a ladder, placing the rock in its designated row. It is a Greek Revival-inspired 1½ story oolitic limestone house. Originally a

hall-parlor plan, the main entrance would have been on the west façade. In 1880, Isaac E. Allred, a druggist, bought the house. Lester Allred purchased the home in 1937, and sold it in 1939 to Earl and Lorna Jensen. The house was purchased and restored in 1996 by Sara Allred Watson.

Reddick was an 1859 Spring Town settler. He had served in the Nauvoo Legion, the Mormon Battalion, and was a wagon train captain. He served a mission to the Sandwich Islands in 1852, and in 1856 he responded to the call to bring in the Martin and Willie Handcart Companies. Capt. Grant left Reddick with the supplies while he searched for the handcarts knowing he could rely on him. When others were persuaded to return to Salt Lake, Reddick refused to leave, so the supplies were on hand when they found the starving pioneers. He was Bishop in Chester.

NO. 48
Jens C. Andersen Home, c. 1884
91 East 100 South

Jens C. Andersen, a Danish immigrant, built this 1½ story brick house. It was constructed of locally fired bricks from a brickyard west of town. The original section was a hall-parlor plan; the matching brick addition was added in 1995. Jens also built the similar brick home at 325 East Center #57, which was later purchased by his son, Christian Andersen.

Jens and Kristen Andersen joined the "Mormon" Church and came to Utah in 1863, settling in Spring Town in 1868. Kristy died not long after their arrival in October 1864, and he then married Ane Olsen. Jens died in 1895, and the tax records show that his son, Christian, owned this home in 1897. He was also taxed for two cows and two horses.

Christian had married Jannette, a daughter of Reddick N. Allred, and this is the home where they raised their family.

NO. 49
Rasmus Jensen Home, c. 1900
116 South 100 West

This one story stuccoed brick hall-parlor house has an original rear kitchen. It was likely built by Rasmus Jensen in 1900. The pedimented portico is a later addition. The house was restored in the late 1990s by Ron Henriksen, and a more recent addition has increased the size of the home.

The "hall-parlor" house is found in 19th century England and colonial North America. It had been developed from the medieval "hall house" where entry of the home leads directly into a one-room hall, or general-purpose room. The "hall-parlor" home has an adjoining smaller room, or a more private parlor.

NO. 50
Andrew Olsen Home, c. 1884
90 South 100 West

Andrew Olsen, a Danish emigrant, came to Utah in 1854. This substantial 1½ story hall-parlor house was built for Olsen in the mid-1880s. He was a farmer and had two wives. The Olsens later moved to Canada. In 1890 the house was sold to Jane Beck. In the late 1990s the house was acquired and restored by the Mitch Burton family. The other structures are more recent. It is currently owned by the Penrods.

The front door was originally on the south, but recent residents use the east door on the rear wing. The south façade opening arrangement is unusual, but

does occur in older houses in Sanpete. This house had five downstairs openings topped by a threesome above. The upstairs door and windows are spaced either directly above or exactly between lower openings to preserve a very sophisticated sense of bilateral tripartite symmetry. The window heads are pedimented. This substantial brick home is one of the most pleasing examples of late 19th century vernacular buildings in Spring City. A small addition at the west does not detract from the original structure.

NO. 51
Robert Blain Home, c. 1883
73 West Center

Robert Blain built this 1½ story, hall-parlor house in 1883. The exterior, shiplap siding was locally planed at Ole Petersen's mill. Robert was a brother of

William and John Blain, the sons of Isabella Graham Blain, known as the "yeast lady." He crossed the Plains with his brother, William, in 1862. Their mother and her other children came to Utah in 1863. Robert married Jane Slack and Melissa Barney. He was a farmer, and in 1877 he began working for the Spring City Co-op as a clerk, working his way to manager. He was also a school trustee and served two terms as postmaster. In 1894, he served a Mission to Great Britain.

The Baxter Mercantile began about 1895 in one room of Baxter's small home on Second North until his trade increased sufficiently to build the store on the corner of Second North and Main #73. Later, Robert Blain partnered in business with Baxter, but he was forced to retire from the retail business when he became blind. However, Robert lived to the advanced age of 83.

No. 52
Bishop's Storehouse, 1905
95 East Center

In 1905, Spring City received one of five new Bishop's storehouses that were built in the Sanpete valley.  Fountain Green, Manti, Fairview and Ephraim also received a new Bishop's storehouse from this standard plan. These buildings were initially constructed to receive tithing in cash and produce, and to store ward records. This storehouse was built of stone and brick under a pyramidal roof with a corner entry framed by low rounded arches. Special meetings were held here in later years. Large granaries, a cellar and barn were also built on this lot to store donated produce.

Seminary was held in the old Bishop's storehouse for those in the 9th grade attending Jr. High. In 1934 and 1935 the Tithing Office was designated as the Relief Society Hall when the old Adobe Meetinghouse showed definite signs of deterioration. Sunday eggs were gathered to aid in the remodeling of this building. Many Relief Society meetings were held here including welfare activities, quilting, as well as canning projects and other functions. It was then used by the DUP until sold to a private owner.

NO. 53
Freeman Allred Home, 1912
121 East Center

This 1½ story brick pattern book house is the only early house in Spring City to sit diagonally upon the lot. The gables and dormers contain decorative wooden shingle patterns. It was built in 1912 for Freeman Allred, a surveyor. He claimed that Spring City was not laid out to the true compass points, and

so he built his house on what he said were the true north-south lines. Indeed, a map of Spring City shows the highway through town follows a northeasterly direction rather than north.

The lot belonged to Matilda Allred who was the widow of Freeman's grandfather, Isaac Allred, who died in 1870. When Matilda died in 1900, Freeman handled the estate and got the property, building the home about 1912. The Freeman Allred family moved to Idaho before 1940; the home was sold to Freeman's brother-in-law, Joseph Franklin Hansen who lived there for many years.

No. 54
Spring City Public School, 1899
45 South 100 East

Late in 1899 a large two-story red-brick building was completed which consolidated the smaller schools. The bricks were light red in color with darker red bricks furnishing the trim over each of the 64 windows, doors and the front entrance. It had eight large rooms with a spacious hallway on each floor and a wide circular stairway connecting the floors. Each schoolroom was equipped with its own large pot-bellied stove which had to be fed often to keep out winter's chill. Eight grades were located in the eight classrooms, with one through four on the first floor and five through eight on the second floor. This elementary school was used for classes until 1957; its classroom doors were shut in 1959. It fell into such a state of disrepair, it was sold it to the Daughters of Utah Pioneers to be used as a museum in 1977. A Restoration Committee was formed, and the community worked forty years to restore this building. It was later sold to the City, and the Friends of

Historic Spring City was formed to continue the restoration. It was dedicated in 2017 as a Community Center.

No. 55
Spring City Junior High School, 1916
150 East Center

Located east of the old Spring City Elementary School, this new white brick building was constructed in 1916 to serve as the Spring City Junior High School and housed 7th, 8th, and 9th graders. One room of the old elementary school became available for use as a Manual Arts or "Shop" area for Junior High students. The new building contained four large rooms, a small library room, and lavatory facilities on the west end, along with a fine gymnasium and stage. Three rooms were used for the three grades and the fourth used for a music or band room.

When the old 1899 Elementary building closed its doors in 1957, this building served as the Elementary School with classes beginning in 1959 until the new Elementary School was built in 1986. It was then purchased by Spring City Corp for city offices until June 2017 when the 1899 Elementary School was restored and opened as a Community Center and new city offices. A variety of Spring City community groups and Senior Citizens utilize this building.

No. 56
Johannes & Caisa Lisa Jonsson Home, 1899
20 South 200 East

This house has been altered considerably over the years. Dr. Carter described it as a hipped roof pattern book house; the original house had a front gable. It

had been altered too severely to contribute to the historical nature of Spring City. However, an old photo of the original home is available. Some of the homes in Spring City that were built of adobes are still in use, although most of them have been covered with stucco or other materials as insurance against deterioration.

The family of John Peter Johnson first lived in a cellar near the northeast corner of the lot. A canal, commonly known as the "big ditch," runs through the lot. It carried water for irrigation to the fields west and north of town, and even for culinary purposes. Then, they built this one room 14'x16' adobe house, roofed with slabs and mud.

NO. 57
Andersen-Madsen Home, c. 1882
325 East Center

This house was built about 1882 by Jens C. Andersen, a Dane. It is a 1½ story brick house with a rear "T" addition. The main portion of the house contains a second story door above a small porch and is built with multi-colored brick. The prominent brick round-arched lintels above the door and window opening in contrast to the brick color of the exterior walls suggest the brick may have come from the same kiln as the brick used for the 1899 Spring City School. (Jens also built the brick home at 91 E 100 S, #48.) He sold the house to his son Christian Andersen for $500 in 1885. [Anders] Christian was the adopted son of Jens C. and Kristy Anderson. When he was a small

child, his poor mother allowed her childless friends, Jens and Kristy, to adopt him and take him to America.

The home was sold in 1891, to Andrew Madsen, a handcart pioneer from Denmark and a Blackhawk War veteran. He was involved with the Spring City Roller Mill. A kitchen addition was constructed in 1910. More recent owners have added more living space.

No. 58
Niels Peter Jensen Home, c. 1880
427 East Center

The Niels Peter Jensen home was built about 1880. It is built of adobe, a rectangular cabin type with three opening façade and internal partition which contains a stove flue chimney. The adobe bricks were originally plastered red and marked off to simulate brick masonry. (It was stuccoed about 1960.) It has a hip roof porch on the front with nicely turned spindle decoration. An addition was added to the east to give

the owners more space. This home is still owned by a descendant of Niels P. Jensen.

Niels Peter "Baker" Jensen came here about 1877; he operated his own bakery in Denmark until government confiscation occurred, after which his family came to Utah. His granddaughter, Christie Beck, remembered that he made his own powdered sugar from granulated sugar and would make beautifully decorated cakes for his friends. He once made a beautiful cake for President Lorenzo Snow who was visiting the Manti Temple.

NO. 59
James C. & Martha Pedersen Home, c. 1910
74 North 300 East

The "Jimmy King" Pedersen house is a 1½ story, brick Victorian pattern book design and one of the most elaborate in Spring City. Work on the house began in the early 1900s, and was completed in 1910. He was successful in the sheep business and this home is a reflection of his high standard of living.

A young man of 22 when he emigrated, he herded sheep and took his pay in sheep to build up his own herd, then sent for his  mother and sisters in Denmark. In 1907, while on an LDS mission to Norway, he met Martha Gabrielsen; she emigrated, and they were married in the Manti Temple and raised seven children.

There are several versions as to how James arrived at this nickname; possibly it was because of his economic prominence in the Danish (northern) section of town and his love of fine clothes, James received the nickname "King." Others maintain that he was tagged with the name when he returned from his LDS mission and married Martha, calling her his "Queen."

NO. 60
John Thomas Blain Home, c. 1895
110 North 200 East

John T. and Christena (Peterson) Blain purchased this lot and were raising their young family in a two-room log home with a dirt roof when John T. decided to build a new house. He hauled oolite stone from the stone quarry hills for the foundation of his home. He worked for two summers hauling lumber from the mill to Nephi; it would take him two days to make the trip. He took his pay in lumber for his home. Carpenters were scarce, and since there was only one carpenter in town who could do the building, it took more than a year to put up the frame work. This 1½ story wooden frame home is a pattern book "L" plan with a gable façade and door on the side wing.

The next winter a tramp came to their door, was invited in and while they were visiting, he told them he was a mason by trade and looking for work. John T. employed him to adobe-line the inside rooms of the house, for which he received a small wage and room and board for the winter.

John T. set up a barber shop in one room of the house, and later sold ice cream on Sunday nights—in the same room, 10¢ a dish.

NO. 6I
Grain Cleaning Shed
60 East IOO North

Sanpete retained claim to the "Granary of Utah" and produced about 80,000 bushels of grain. After the

wheat was threshed, it had to be cleaned. One early method of grain cleaning entailed spreading a canvas on the ground on a windy day, pouring the grain onto the canvas and letting the wind blow away the chaff. Andrew Bradley and wife, Leanie, began cleaning wheat and other grain with a hand-turned fan which would blow out the chaff as the crank was turned—a very slow, hard method. Neither method removed the "smut" contaminants.

James William Schofield responded to farmers' needs by cleaning their grain for them for the small fee of 10¢ with a machine mounted on a one-horse dray on which the machine was loaded and taken to each farmer needing the service.

Some years later, Will built a building to house his cleaning machine and obtained an elevator which carried the grain from the wagon to the top of the machine where it could proceed through the screens to be cleaned. This machine still stands in its building, ready to be used at any time.

No. 62
Hans Jorgen Hansen Home,
92 North 200 East

Built about 1874, this house is of Scandinavian design, a "parstuga' or "pair house. It is one of only three still in town. It was built of stone and later given a stuccoed exterior.

Hans and Anne were married in 1847, and Hans at one time was an "expert gardener of repute" who trained in the Royal Gardens of the King of Denmark.

Hans and his son, Hemming #80 walked across the plains, bringing their possessions in a light wagon pulled by a team of oxen in 1859. At first, they lived in a dugout in Spring Town, which was replaced with a log home. Still later, the larger rock home was built which is where Roger and Lila Allred raised their family. Their daughter, Julie Allred, now lives here and has undertaken to remove the stucco from the exterior and return the home to the original stone.

The northeast boundary marker for Spring Town can still be seen near this home to show what was once the city limits of the town. It also has a much more practical purpose—it keeps people from cutting the corner and driving on their lawn.

NO. 63
Danish Meetinghouse, 1863
119 East 100 North

The stone marker on the corner of Hans Jorgen's lot is catty-corner to the location of where the adobe Danish meetinghouse was built. Eventually, the beams

were used in another building and sometime after 1951 the adobe bricks melted away and returned to the earth.

During the October Conference 1853, Bishop R.W. Allred and his father, James, requested more families be sent to the settlement to bolster their numbers against the threat of Ute Warriors. About one-half of the newly arrived company of 297 Scandinavians left for Sanpete; 50 families joined the Allred settlement and congregated on the north side of town which later became known as "Little Denmark." Amidst a certain amount of animosity, lack of communication, different customs and habits, misunderstandings and misplaced prejudice, it is understandable that these people would seek their own and feel the need to gather to worship in their own language. The Danish attended Sacrament meetings in the Main Street church, but met here for Sunday School, to sing and make merry, and also for school classes. The Danish meetinghouse was still used as late as the 1920s and 30s.

NO. 64
Lars & Petrea (Monson) Larsen Home, c. 1883
85 North 100 East

This large stone house, built by Peter Monson, is a distinctively Scandinavian type known as a "parstuga" or pair house consisting of a three-room-wide floor plan. The east façade contains a central gable above the second story door and the entry. The large  stone rear addition to the west gives it the appearance of a cross-wing house. The large upstairs room was often used for dancing.

Monson came from Sweden and was a miller by trade, and a builder of windmills. He had gone to Norway as a young man to operate a mill and while there he met Bertha Bouse. They had a long 10-year courtship and dreamed of going to America; arriving in 1859, they settled in Spring City where he helped make the first grist mill, but later turned to farming. In 1861, a baby girl was born to them, Petrea, their only child. When this little girl was two years old, a great tragedy came into her life when she fell into the open fireplace sustaining serious burns to her face and body. Peter prospered and built this fine stone house for his daughter and son-in-law, Lars Larsen.

No. 65
School Teacher's Home/Methodist School
55 East 100 North

The Methodist chapel and school building was erected about 1887-1889. The main goal of the Church at the time was to improve the education levels of children throughout Utah, which it was successful in doing. Once the home of the Methodist school teacher or minister, this home has recently been added onto to the east where the school was once attached to the house. This was a fine lumber structure with a large bell in the tower atop it, and grades one through eight were taught in one large room. Several older residents remember that parties in the Methodist school were very special and that neighborhood children were invited even though they were not pupils. The church-school section has been torn down for many years.

 About 1915, Methodist school enrollment had dropped and closure became imminent. Minister "Merk" donated the beautiful sounding bell to the 1899 Public School, a generous and much appreciated gift.

NO. 66
Behunin-Beck Home, 1883
19 East 100 North

This large two-story home was built by Isaac M.
Behunin in
1883. A stone
plaque inserted
into the top
gabled dormer
on the west
façade reads
"Erected by

Behunnin, 1883." When Isaac was age 20 the family
became the first settlers of Ephraim prior to the
Walker War and the 1853 evacuations to Manti. He
was a blacksmith, and also something of a dentist and
doctor. He also served as Mayor, Councilman, and
Justice of the Peace. He sold the home to Simon T.
Beck for $1200 in 1887. Beck arrived in Spring Town
in 1863 and figured very prominently in the Spring
City scene for many years beginning in the cattle
business, and then later building a sheep herd to a
reported 3500 in 1897, with many acres of land.

The Beck home is one of the most nostalgic spots
in Spring City's history. Charlie, the son of Simon
Beck, had a bench the women of town called the
"Bummer's Bench." Charlie fell victim to typhoid
fever and meningitis; paralyzed from the waist down at
age 19; he presided at the bench for 32 years
"providing advice and wisdom to all comers."

NO. 67
William Downard Home, 1890-1900
165 West 100 North

This house was supposedly built by William Downard, the son of George Downard #46, between 1890 and 1900. It is a frame hall-parlor house type commonly found in Spring City. The façade has a three opening symmetrical appearance and the stove chimneys are placed at gable ends. The house appears to be considerably altered; asphalt shingles, siding and larger windows have been added by 1978. Despite the alterations this house certainly dates from the later 19th century and points to the longevity of folk building practices in Spring City.

Phyllis (Sorensen) Blain remembered her grandma lived in this home and Phyllis would deliver vegetables to her. The home was in pretty rough shape, but was purchased in 2003 and the property has been gradually revamped in this lovely setting.

NO. 68
John F. Bohlin Home, 1884
138 North 100 West

John Bohlin (Bohleen) and his wife lived in this stuccoed adobe house; a single room was built about 1859. John was a stonemason for many buildings in Spring City, however, it isn't known if he built this house. He owned the lot until 1874, but it is believed

the Bohlin family lived in another location, and then moved back to this home where his wife died and later his daughter. John Bohlin contributed to the beautiful stone work of the Manti Temple and later used his talents in the supervision of our Spring City Chapel construction, as well as in the building of the City Hall.

John Bohlin had a good friend, Andrew Johnson (Johansen) who had been in Utah for just over a year when he was killed in the Ute raid in 1867. He was a convert from Sweden with two daughters, and his wife, Johanna (Johnson), was expecting their third child. He lingered though the day, and asked his good friend, John, to promise to care for his widow-to-be and his two daughters. He kept that promise and later married Johanna and had a son of their own.

NO. 69a
Emil Erickson Home, 1888
119 West 200 North

Emil Erickson, a Swedish immigrant, was a carpenter and worked with masons J. P. Carlson and John Bohlin to build this 1½ story Victorian eclectic cross-wing house, with fish scale shingles in the gables. It was constructed of oolitic rubble stone which was coursed and pointed with raised mortar to approximate cut stone masonry. Craig and M'Lisa Paulsen restored the house in the 1970s adding an adjacent stone cabin and furnace room. Emil also worked on the Manti Temple and the rock Chapel.

NO. 69b
Peter Jensen Home, 1870s
151 West 200 North

Dr. Tom Carter preserved this cabin as one of the few remaining Norwegian log houses in Utah, perhaps the last one. It was moved here from Central, Utah, and he rebuilt it in 1987.

It is noteworthy for the "key" or tongued notch joint at the corners. It is so well made that chinking is not required between the logs.

NO. 70
Ephraim Larsen Home, c. 1884
II2 West 200 North

Ephraim Larsen built this one-story home about 1884. The concrete block addition was added in 1950.

They had chickens, pigs and several cows and a large vegetable garden. "Eph" was the son of Johannes and Anna Jorgensen Larsen, born in Spring Town in 1860. He married Diantha Justesen, the daughter of Lars Alexander Justesen (who was a war casualty, killed in Sevier in the 1868) and Jensine Mathilda Jensen, and the sister of Matilda Frances Justesen (who was the wife of Judge Jacob Johnson).

Eph became the manager for Judge Johnson's 600 acre farm up Canal Canyon; they lived in the small rock homestead house on that property. He died in 1905 of Rocky Mountain Spotted Fever leaving Diantha and six little girls. They moved back to this little rock house where she attempted to raise them, with a lot of family help and doing work as a dressmaker. She was always sewing for her sister Matilda and the girls, who was very generous and saw to it that she was well paid.

NO. 71
Alex Justesen-Watson Home, 1898
187 North Main

The plan of this house is an upside down "T" with the base or stem of the "T" a forward projecting gable. This front gable is beveled to resemble a bay window. Shingling in the gables lends a decorative touch. There were three rooms and a loft in the early days of the house, with a 1916 addition of kitchen and bathroom. Built about 1898 by Alex Justesen,  whose wife divorced him about 1901. The granary was built around the same time with a tack room addition later. The current barn replaced an older barn. It was purchased by William E. Watson about 1909, and is still in Watson ownership. The garage was added when Mr. Watson purchased a vehicle.

Many vagrants found their way to Spring City from the railroad station to beg a bowl of soup or a piece of bread. Will Watson was one man who would never turn anyone away hungry, but he always insisted that some chores be completed before the man left so that he could feel some pride. Older residents insist that the beggars had a special system of marking a gatepost in front of indulgent homes so that future beggars could also receive a handout.

NO. 72
John R. Baxter, Sr. Home, 1903
12 West 200 North

John R. Baxter Sr., mayor from 1894-1895, was a prosperous merchant and built this Victorian 1½ story house as a tribute to his success in 1903 diagonally across Main Street from his store. Jens Peter Carlson, a local mason, did much of the masonry work. It is a good example of Victorian pattern book design and illustrates influences of the Queen Anne style with gable shingling and an ornate spindled porch. The family rented rooms while they lived in the house. It was designed to accommodate a 4'x4'x4' lead-lined cistern on the second floor to provide water pressure to the first floor. The Baxter family owned the house

 until 1985. It was restored in the 1990s, and more recently, condemned after

sustaining extensive water damage, but was saved by our historic contractor, Craig Paulsen.

John R. Baxter was born in 1851 in Scotland coming to Spring City in 1869. He worked at farming and for the railroad until he went with Samuel Allred in 1872 to help with the construction of the St. George Temple.

NO. 73
Baxter Store, c. 1895
190 North Main

This stone and wood frame façade building is the best surviving example of 19th century commercial architecture in Spring City.

John R. Baxter, Sr. first opened a store in his house on the same lot. Later, the business became known as Baxter and Blain Mercantile. Upon Baxter's death in 1930, the store was acquired by his son-in-law and renamed the Schofield Mercantile. The Squirt signs painted on the façades date from the 1940s.

John had attended the University of Deseret, graduating in 1876, and returned to Spring City to teach until he was called on a two-year mission to Scotland. After John married Jannett Jack, the daughter of a missionary companion, they settled in Spring City where he owned a farm and some sheep. He worked in the Co-op Store until he branched out in his own mercantile business becoming one of the more affluent families.

The Baxters played an important part in the building of Spring City beyond the pioneering era.

NO. 74
Petersen-Nielsen Home, c. 1880
15 East 200 North

This fine old adobe house is interesting because of the elaborate porch decoration, patterned gable shingling, and simulated stone plastering. It is a cross-wing house covered with scored stucco simulating stone. The house was originally built by Ole Petersen who sold out to Hans Nielsen in 1882. Nielsen was a farmer and a stockholder in the Young Men's Co-op Store. Nielsen built the many outbuildings which are found on the lot.

Ole Petersen was born in Denmark in 1849 and was an early resident of Fort Ephraim. In 1864 Petersen was called to settle Circle Valley, after which he located in Spring City in 1873. Petersen served three terms as Mayor and also as a City Councilman. He built the Spring City Planing Mill in 1891. After the death of his first wife, Ida Neilson, Petersen married Anna Backman Neilsen (Anna Billington) who was a local mid-wife of special note. The Petersens moved to Idaho because of Ole's poor health, and then later part of the family returned to Spring City.

NO. 75
Jens Petersen Home, c. 1874
147 North 100 East

Jens Petersen, a weaver from Denmark, built the front two rooms of this one story stone house in 1874. By 1882 the house was owned by Orson Allred and in 1935 it was sold to Vera Downard Sorensen. A fire and subsequent restoration resulted in an addition to the north and west of the original structure in 1981. A log barn at the rear of the lot has also been restored.

Jens was a farmer and a cooper, or a maker of casks and barrels, in Spring City, then moved to go to Carbon County after 1880. He was a Blackhawk War veteran. His daughter, Mary, remained in Spring City and married William H. Schofield, and then later married John Robinson, Jr. Jens returned to Spring City and died in the home of his daughter, but is buried in Price beside his wife. Current owners are George and Lois Kenzy.

NO. 76
N. Peter & Olene (Olsen) Hansen Home, c. 1874
192 North 200 East

This 1½ story brick house was constructed by Niels Peter Hansen in the mid-1870s. It is a hall-parlor plan with a rear addition. Hansen, an immigrant from Denmark, and a Blackhawk War veteran, settled in Spring City in 1860. They owned this house until

1890. He is the brother of Hemming Hansen #80 who built his house nearby and the son of Hans Jorgen Hansen whose home was at 92 N 200 E, #62. His father accepted the contract to carry mail between Spring City and Ephraim. The last two mail carriers had been killed by "Indians," so no one was anxious to take the job. Hans said he and his 16-year old son, Niels Peter, would do it. Near Pigeon Hollow, riding through the cedar trees, the "Indians" would lie in wait to ambush him. His faithful little mare always sensed their presence and avoided them. He would give the mare her head and she would race through the Hollow, the disappointed "Indians" with wild war whoops raced after him. When he was far enough away, he would rein up and wave while they brandished their weapons.

Mette C. Christoffersen Home, c. 1881
191 North 300 East

This one-story adobe house was built about 1881 by Hans and Mette Kristine "Stena" (Nielsen) Christoffersen. The roofing system is a heavy timber technique with axe-hewn rafters that is rarely found in Sanpete. The home follows the Scandinavian tradition

of placing the chimney in the center of the home rather than in the gable ends. It was stuccoed and then painted to imitate red brick as late as 1950, but has since been painted over. Hans Peter Christoffersen inherited the home in 1919, and then subsequently sold it to his sister Margaret Sorensen. It is now owned by Ron and Becky Tucker.

Hans Peter, who married Delila Clawsen, was the Christophersen's first child to be born in America, 1880. He lived in Spring City his whole life and was a sheepherder and farmer. Margaret married William H. Sorensen in 1910, but they didn't have any children. Will was a foreman in the Deseret Livestock operation, and she reportedly mothered the young men who were employees. It was said of her that "she played a great and romantic role in the pioneering of the Company."

NO. 78
Jens Severine Jensen Home, c. 1879
276 North 300 East

Jens built this 1½ story adobe hall-parlor house in the 1870s. Originally, the 12" thick adobe walls were whitewashed; the home was always cool in the summer and warm in the winter. There is milled spindle work on the porch. The barn is from c. 1875, the granary c. 1890. A cellar under the north room had its access through a bedroom, and the attic was accessed through an outside stairway. Eight of Jens and Maria's nine children were born here. After Maria's death, the home came into the possession of their son  George who added a kitchen to the back of the house and a storage room on the north side. After Spring City installed the water system in 1935, a bathroom was added to the east side of the house. The home remained in the Jensen family until 1972 when it was purchased by Michael Sorensen. The house was stuccoed and painted with bright red lines imitating brick, but is now covered with siding.

Jens arrived in Utah about 1871 with his widowed mother, Jensine, who married Iver Peter Petersen #84, his brother Charles Marinus #90 and his sister Mary.

NO. 79
Olsen-Jensen Home, c. 1870
269 East 300 North

The exact origin of this home is uncertain, although Andrew N. Olsen most likely built the western log portion. It was probably constructed about 1870 of hewn logs joined at the corners with a "V" notch. The adobe portion on the east side was built later after 1881 by Mathias Jensen. It is apparent the log section was made taller when the addition was roofed and  the porch added as can be seen by the dovetail corner notching of the upper logs.

NO. 80
Hemming Edward Hansen Home, c. 1894
288 North 200 East

When Hemming arrived in Salt Lake with his parents, Hans Jergen and Anne Hansen #62 in 1859, he enlisted in the territorial militia against the Indians. He also worked as a freighter until the late 1860s when

he moved to Spring City. He built this wood frame, cross-wing house about 1894. The wood siding was obtained locally from Ole Petersen's mill. His brother, Niels Peter Hansen, built his house nearby #76. Hemming was a farmer, a city councilman, city water master, and director of the Horseshoe Irrigation Co. He served a mission in Scandinavia in 1885, and his missionary diary is on display in the Old School Museum. He sold everything he could to raise the money necessary to go. When he arrived in Copenhagen, the Mormon missionaries were being banished, but because Hemming had been born on Danish soil and was a citizen, he was allowed to remain in Denmark. When he returned to Spring City, he homesteaded some land where he planted trees for lumber; he farmed the land and raised grain. He became an avid gardener in later years.

NO. 81
Old Spring City Pioneer Cemetery
240 North 100 East

This cemetery was used until 1869 when the cemetery west of town was started. There are 67 known burials including three Blackhawk War casualties, a handcart pioneer, and many children;

many deaths from sickness, poor conditions, bad drinking water, and epidemics.

The exact date of the first burial in the Pioneer Cemetery is unknown. It is believed that the earliest death was Newton Devine Allred who died in 1857, although the settlers were not here at that time while the last burial was Isaac Morton Behunin who died January 4, 1910 (he is buried near his wife who had died years earlier).

This cemetery was full of graves. The west end was nearly covered with wooden markers, but due to vandalism and animals being used to keep the weeds down, these and others have been broken and lost. Some graves were marked with only a square stone at the head and a smaller one at the foot, and still others were of sandstone, and if there ever were any names, dates, etc., time and the elements have erased them.

NO. 82
Sorensen's Barn
245 North 100 East

This rock barn may be the only example left of a Scandinavian barn. Just as the homes of the Scandinavian settlers differed from other settlers, their barns also varied in construction. The non-Scandinavian settlers generally laid logs horizontally, notching each end to form the four walls. Scandinavians usually built a frame and attached planks vertically.

Outbuildings were constructed in close proximity to the home or were sometimes attached. Rock appeared more typically in Scandinavian outbuildings and is symbolic of the especially fine treatment Danes lavished on their livestock. It is said it was the Danish custom that milking cows was firmly delegated to the women and children of the household, and the barn was washed down every day. Woven willow fences were erected, but were not widespread.

No. 83
Frederick Olsen Home, c. 1875
298 North Main

The old Olsen house shows up in early photos as one of the best stone house examples in Spring City, particularly reminiscent of the smaller homes built at Nauvoo. This stone house is a 1½ story rectangle cabin with an inside partition with stove flue chimneys located in the gables. A frame one room square cabin with three-opening façade has been moved in and connected to the main house on the east by a frame passageway. There is also a summer kitchen and a granary.

In 1868, Frederick Olson became Spring Town's second Bishop after the resettlement. Up until the town was incorporated in 1870, the Ward Bishop assumed control of things of common interest such as canyon road building, public fencing, etc. He was Bishop, then called to Emery County in 1882 were he stayed. He died in 1906 in Ferron and is buried there.

NO. 84
Iver Peter Petersen Home, c. 1875
309 North Main

Iver Petersen, a Danish immigrant, built this oolite stone, hall-parlor plan house in the mid-1870s using cast off stone from the temple. Each family worked a day building the temple, and the rubble stone was available for the workers' use. A rear adobe addition was constructed shortly thereafter. A stone granary behind the house has been made into a living space where the current owner often holds organ recitals.

Iver and his brother Ole Petersen #74 moved to Spring City after the war. He married Caroline Mortensen and had 7 children before Iver died at the age of 37 leaving his wife a widow for 54 years. He had been a freighter which left Caroline responsible for the farm and animals much of the time.

He was also a cooper making wooden barrels for storing food, feed, and supplies. After his death, Caroline supported herself by storing grain. As the farmers deposited their grain in her granary, she would put slash marks on the wall by the door keeping record of the farmers' deposits.

No. 85
Peter Justesen Home, c. 1887
85 West 400 North

This 1½ story stone house was constructed by Peter Justesen after 1885. It was probably his second house in Spring City as he also built the house located at 428 South 100 West #29 about 1876. This house was built with one room and a rear lean-to.

In 1889 it was sold to Sidney R. Allred and then Jens Hansen. Several new additions have been added to the rear.

Sidney R. Allred was the son of Isaac and Mary Allred. His father often played the violin, many times in the home of the Prophet Joseph Smith, and Sidney remembered well sitting on his lap.

When Sidney married Lucy their first home was on Alvin Allred's lot and all they had for a door was a quilt. It wasn't until sometime later when Elder Orson Hyde came to "eat baked potatoes with us" that he gave him some nails and some material to hang a door, "did the quilt come down to help us with a warmer bed."

NO. 86
Peter & Aninia Mickel Home & Cabin, 1900
389 North 100 East

This small brick pattern book, cross-wing house was erected for Peter P. and Anna Allred Mickel. It is one of the best examples of pattern book architecture remaining in Spring City and is historically significant as the best preserved later 19th/early 20th century smaller home in town. "Pattern book" houses were well-developed architectural styles that were popular throughout America in the 19th and early 20th century. They could easily be adapted by local builders according to local building traditions. This home is balanced by front porches; notice, in particular, the spindled porch work.

Peter P. and Anenia (Anna) Mickel were the owners in 1900, but due to some problems Peter was having with the law at the time, Anna Mickel sold the home to Hans Nielsen and Frank Crawforth in 1901 for $1000, which was deeded back to Anna in 1902—for $10. Anna then sold the home to Mary Sorensen for $500 in 1903. David H. and Mary (Rasmussen) Sorensen raised their family in this home. Her parents

were Peter and Kristine Rasmussen across the street #87. It was enlarged in the 1990s.

NO. 87
Peter & Kristine Rasmussen Home, c. 1878
378 North 100 East

Peter Rasmussen bought this lot from his father, Christian, in 1878 for $14 and erected this 1½ story stone house for his wife Kristina Larsen. It is a traditional hall-parlor plan typical of the Scandinavian architecture, with a rear addition. The Danes especially loved to dance and Peter's home was one of the homes that had an upstairs room large enough to be considered a ballroom for dancing.

Peter and Kirsten were converts from Denmark and came to America with their small family in 1863. While crossing the plains, one of their children wandered away and was never seen again, although the camp waited four days while they frantically searched for the child. Three children died that year, and they started their family over again in Fairview, Utah. The family lived in Spring City by 1867, and by the 1870 census, the couple had a young family of three children. Of the couple's 14 children, only 5 outlived their parents, most died young.

Peter was a participant in the Blackhawk War.

 Some of the family lived in this home for many years.

NO. 88
Lorenzo Aiken Home, c. 1908
Service Station, 1924
488 North Main

Lorenzo Wilson Aiken, a sheep shearer, and his wife, Mary Jane (Nielson) Aiken, built this small corner service station in 1924. It was the first station built in Spring City. Mary Jane and their small children ran the  station during the years of 1928-29 to keep Lorenzo in the mission field to the eastern states. Later, Lorenzo and Mary Jane's son, Denzel Aiken, ran the station. The last person to run the station sold Shell and Wasatch gasoline. The c. 1908 pattern book brick house behind the station replaced a small log house. The house has a pyramid roof and round arched corbeling above the windows and doors.

Aiken's service station, the first station in town built to sell gas and oil, was not in the "downtown  area." It had several operators, then closed about 1941.

NO. 89
Andrew & Sena Munk Thompsen Home, c. 1886
488 North 200 East

This one story adobe hall-parlor house with rear addition was built after 1886 for Andrew and Sena Munk (Jensen) Thompsen who emigrated from Denmark. They raised ten children here. Later, after the parents left the LDS Church and became Seventh Day Adventists, they often held meetings in their  home. The house was restored in 1997 and the adobe was stuccoed and scored to look like brick.

"Fish" Thompson received his nickname because of his periodic fishing trips to Utah Lake and others, after which he would peddle his catch through Spring City streets with his little four-colored cock-eyed mongrel yipping and whirling to let people know he was coming. "Fish" also operated a "smoke house" for those who wished to take advantage of his services and had no smoke house of their own.

One of the earliest and perhaps largest "adobe yards" was the Thompson family "yard" which was located on Oak Creek about 300 East and 800 North. Anders (Andrew) "Fishman" Thompson was involved in this operation as well as carpentry. Adobes sold for $5.00 per thousand.

NO. 90
Marinus Petersen Home, c. 1878
285 East 500 North

Charles Marinus Jensen-Petersen, arrived in Utah about 1871 from Denmark and built this rock house and barn for his family. The hall-parlor, 1½ story house has a symmetrical façade pierced by three openings. In 1924 a hipped roof addition was added to the rear. The house remains one of the outstanding 19th century rock homes in Spring City.

Marinus and his wife Almina (Christensen) had 11 children, but only five lived to adulthood. He was a farmer, and his brother Jens Severine Jenson lived

nearby at 276 N 300 E, # 78. His son, Marvin, or "Bish," was a bachelor and lived in the rock home after the death of his parents until his death in 1978. His nickname stands for "Bishop" and is a tongue-in-cheek reference to Petersen's strictly non-Mormon attitude. There is an adjacent hay barn with log crib and frame stable; other outbuildings on the site have been remodeled for extra living space. It is currently owned by Randall and Sherry Thatcher.

No. 91
Iver & Maria Christensen Home, c. 1908
323 East 500 North

Iver Christensen completed this 1½ story folk house with a two-opening, window-door-façade about 1908. It had leaded windows and relieving arched surrounds. The upstairs loft was reached by a staircase located outside on the north side. The house is a single cell building with a rear lean-to addition. The adjacent summer kitchen was remodeled into a bath and connected by a breezeway to the house. A log cabin was moved onto the property and has been remodeled.

Iver was born in Castle Dale, Emery County in 1885 and married Maria Sandstrom in 1901. They began their family in this home, however, the births of their children were interrupted when Iver served in World War I. Upon his safe return, they lived here in Spring City the rest of their lives.

NO. 92
Hansen-Jensen Home, c. 1892
385 East 500 North

This brick pattern book house was most likely built by Jens Hansen and later sold to Hyrum Jensen, a local farmer. Hyrum Soren Jensen, son of Jene S. Jensen and Maria Magdalene Christensen, was born in Spring City in 1883. He married Myrtle Clawson and they had three children. He served as City Councilman and Mayor for several terms, 1942-1945 and 1950-1953. He died in May, 1967.

"Hy" made an addition to the house as his family grew. In the 1930s the house was surrounded by numerous fruit trees. The Jensen family lived here for many years and thereafter it remained vacant. It was sold in the 1980s, and later purchased and restored by Midge and George Delavan.

Although the town of Spring City is a Historic District on the National Register, the homes are all privately owned and are not open to the public.

Heritage Day is an annual celebratory event held in Spring City the Saturday of Memorial Day weekend. This community event started in 1984 as a fundraiser for the preservation of the historic Spring City Elementary School building. Some of the homes are featured each year in a "Home Tour" on this one day only event.

For information about the annual home tour program, please visit the Friends of Historic Spring City website. www.historicspringcity.com

If you would like to schedule a tour with a volunteer, please contact the City offices:

435-462-2244
SpringCityUtah.org

Works Cited

Hyde, Myrtle Stevens. *Orson Hyde: Olive Branch of Israel.*
    Agreka Books, 2000.

Watson, Kaye C. *Life Under the Horseshoe: A History of Spring
    City.* Publishers Press, 1987.

(Additional information is from pioneer "Histories" found
    in the Old City Hall DUP museum library and are
    there for the public to use.)

SPECIAL RECOGNITION

Kaye C. Watson was the editor of *Life Under the Horseshoe*, the history book published for Spring City in 1987. Starting around 1980, Kaye worked with DUP Captain Christie Bunnell, Cynthia Allred, Nedra Allred, Uarda Blackham, Craig Paulsen, Dan Vincent and many other contributors to produce the treasured volume in order to help raise money to restore the 1899 Spring City Elementary School. It was published in conjunction with the Canal and Horseshoe DUP Camps and the Mayors and City Council Members of Spring City during 1984, 1985 and 1986.

Kaye has been an invaluable member of the community with her acquired knowledge of the history of Spring City, its citizens, their homes and historic buildings, and her love of family history research. She is always willing to help others with their research, or provide informational tours in Spring City. Her many years of volunteerism are commendable.

A Pennsylvania native, she attended High School in Maryland, then arriving in Utah to attend LDS Business College and staying to find employment. She met Dennis Watson while working at the Utah Air National Guard, and they later married and had two sons. She has always served in a variety of LDS Church capacities both in Washington DC and Utah. She has also been active in the community joining the North Sanpete chapter of Young Homemakers, being a Republican Mass Meeting Officer and Registration Agent, supporting her husband in his 8 years on the City Council, and teaching DUP lessons; she also worked at the Post Office for 17 years.

When there's extra time she has been involved with the Extraction program, genealogy, playing with the grandkids, keeping in touch with friends and relatives, and helping many people find out more about their ancestors.

INDEX

Made in the USA
Columbia, SC
17 April 2018